Treasures of

SICILIAN
CUISINE

NOTES:

Imperial measurements are given to quantify ingredients.

Wild fennel may be substituted by the tops of bulb fennel.

Some of the listed Italian cheeses may not be easily available. Here is a description of them with a suitable substitute:

Pecorino: it comes in large cylinders with hard yellow rind, and yellowish- white interior. This hard dry cheese is good for grating and used mainly in cooking. It can be used in any recipe that calls for Parmesan cheese, especially if a sharper flavor is desired.

Primosale: a fresh cheese. mozzarella, less compact, can be used instead if a milder flavor is desired.

Caciocavallo: a cheese produced from whole cow milk. Similar to provolone.

Ricotta: a soft, fresh cheese produced from ewe's milk. Similar to cottage cheese.

Pasta "al dente" - [al-DEN-tay]: An Italian phrase meaning "to the tooth" used to describe pasta or other food that is cooked only until it offers a slight resistance when bitten into, but which is not soft or overdone.

Add pasta to the boiling water. Cook for 2 to 5 minutes testing "the bite" from minute to minute, thinner pastas cook faster.

Peeling tomatoes for sauce: Score the flower end of the tomatoes with a small cross. Then immerse the tomatoes in boiling water for 10 seconds. Remove and immerse in ice water. The peel should be easy to remove, starting with the scored end. Cut the tomatoes in half, remove seeds, and rough chop for sauce.

American/British Glossary of terms

- Broil - Grill
- Blender - Liquidizer
- Canned - Tinned
- Celery stalk - Celery stick
- Eggplant - Aubergine
- Legumes - Pulses
- Zucchini - Courgettes

Measurements

- 4 ounces flour = one cup = 125 grams
- 4 ounces butter = one stick = 125 grams
- 7 ounces casted/granulated sugar = one cup = 200 grams
- one ounce = one rounded tablespoon
- 8 fluid ounces = one cup = 250 ml = half a US pint

Abbreviations

- Bu. - bunch
- TT - to taste
- tbsp - tablespoon

TREASURES OF SICILIAN CUISINE

Photographer: Leonardo Frusteri
Chef: Salvatore Fraterrigo
Author: Alba Allotta
Managing editor: Paolo Salerno
Graphic Designer: Salvatore Calìa
Photolith: Pigiemme - Palermo
Printing: Officine Grafiche Riunite
Palermo, April 2009

English edition:

- Translations: Cherida V. Bush
- Consulting Editor: Byron Bush, Graduate of the California Culinary Academy.

Edizione: PS ADVERT   info@psadvert.it • www.psadvert.it • Tel. +39 0923 538789
PROMOLIBRI   Via Aquileia, 84 Palermo • Tel. +39 091 6702413 - Fax +39 091 6703333

Leonardo Frusteri, Salvatore Fraterrigo, Alba Allotta, Paolo Salerno

Treasures of
SICILIAN
CUISINE

a taste of yesterday and today's Mediterranean

PS ADVERT EDIZIONI

PROMOLIBRI

The Publishers

Paolo Salerno advertising agent and Leonardo Frusteri a photographer have this dream in common: to represent the culinary achievements of Sicilians through a new and modern vehicle to reveal colors and tastes of the island. This idea has been cultivated for years, without haste, waiting for the best opportunity. When a Chef Salvatore Fraterrigo and, Alba Allotta, writer and gastronome, joined in the dream become a reality. Chefs, gourmets and foodies, like the publishers, understand the burning passion behind presenting good food or the recipes, photographs and folklore behind it. Researching the best cuisine in the island and creating recipes has been an international effort stretching from Italy, to Canada and the USA. Authentic recipes have been made internationally usable with pictures and translations.

Introduction

The mother of Sicilian cuisine is the island itself: her soil, wind, sun, the Mediterranean. This land has brought it forth. The women and their cleverness to elaborate and make do. In many ways with the same or alternate ingredients. The birth of Sicilian food is somewhere in the cultures of invaders and visitors; Elimi, Phoenicians, Greek, and Romans and more have contributed to a mixture of tastes and aromas.

Evolving still, it is impossible to find just one influence that can take the most credit.

The Arabs, the French, and Spaniards, a cuisine that has reinvented itself with great splendor under every domination, every time.

Each one has left and taken something. Obviously there is a cuisine of the inland areas which presents mainly meat, cheese, vegetables and legumes, and a cuisine of the coastal areas all based on fish. But there is also a pervasive cuisine, simple never poor. The philosophy of "simple" is best is Sicilian as well Italian. As characterized by the serving of plain fruit for dessert. The monsù's, belonging to the French cooks of the island's aristocracy demonstrate knowledge making a full circle in the history.

Enjoy the eclectic recipes and pictures. Then go to the kitchen and cook genuine Sicilian food.

CONTENTS

APPETIZERS

Sicilian tidbits and snacks that farmers today still call "sbrogghia pitittu", whet the appetite and prepare the palate to the seduction of the pleasures of the table. Strong tastes definitely. Some have conformed to the trends of international cuisine which raises appetizers to the role of small gastronomic "solos".
Simple dishes that aim at the desire to eat well. And so together with the traditional rice "arancini" (rice balls), eggplant caponata, panelle (chickpea loaves) and olives, are the tuna botargo, the sweet and sour yellow pumpkin, the couscous taboulè, whitebait pancakes, stuffed artichokes.

"Arancine" (rice balls with meat sauce)

4 servings

2 cups of rice
7 ounces minced meat
1/2 carrot
1/2 onion
1 stalk of celery with leaves
2 tbsp of tomato concentrate
parsley, 1 tuft
3 1/2 ounces of fresh caciocavallo
3 1/2 ounces of shelled peas
4 eggs
1 small bag of saffron
2 tbsp grated Parmesan cheese
1 1/2 cup breadcrumbs
1 cup flour
3 tbsp dry white wine
ounces butter
2 cups extra virgin olive oil
salt, pepper TT

Put the oil, butter and minced onion, celery and carrot in a saucepan. Before the herbs are golden, add the minced meat and sauté for a few minutes; then, sprinkle with a little wine and allow to evaporate. Add the peas and mix for a couple of minutes. Stir in a cup of warm water, to which you will have added the tomato concentrate. Add salt, pepper, minced parsley and simmer for 30 minutes, stirring from time to time. Boil the rice in abundant salted water; strain and put in a bowl. Season it with the saffron, dissolved in a little water, 1 beaten egg and the Parmesan cheese. Let the mixture cool down and put a spoonful in one hand. Squash the rice, and make a shell you will fill with a spoon of the meat sauce and the diced cheese. Close up with some more rice and shape it into a ball. Cover slightly with flour; dip them in the beaten eggs and then in the breadcrumbs and deep fry them in abundant hot vegetable oil. Drip, set on kitchen paper towels to absorb the oil in excess and serve.

Tuna botargo

4 servings

5 ounces tuna botargo (dried and salted tuna eggs)
1 lemon
8 tbsp extra virgin olive oil

Finely slice the botargo and put on a course dish. Trickle with extra virgin olive oil and allow to rest for a few hours.
Before serving remove the oil in excess and add lemon juice.

Sweet and Sour Yellow Pumpkin

4 servings

- **2 pounds** of yellow pumpkin
- **3 cloves** of garlic
- **6 tbsp** extra virgin olive oil
- **5 tbsp** white vinegar
- **1 tbsp** sugar
- salt TT

Clean the pumpkin, remove seeds and skin and cut into slices. Cut each slice into 3 or 4 pieces. Brown the crushed cloves of garlic in a frying pan with oil, then discard and add the pumpkin. Add salt and pepper and fry until brown.
Sprinkle with vinegar, in which you will have dissolved the sugar and boil. Put in a serving dish with the juice and serve it cool.

Eggplant Parmigiana

4 servings

- **5** eggplants
- **2 cups** of tomato sauce
- basil, 1 tuft
- **1** small onion
- **1** clove of garlic
- **5 ounces** of primosale cheese
- **5 tbsp** grated Parmesan cheese
- **3 tbsp** extra virgin olive oil
- **2 cups** vegetable oil
- **1/2** teaspoon sugar
- salt, pepper TT

Crush garlic and sauté in a saucepan with the olive oil and the onion; add the tomato sauce, a handful of leaves of basil, a dash of salt, a dash of pepper and a pinch of sugar. Mix carefully and simmer for about 20 minutes. Remove garlic and onion and keep aside. Wash the eggplants and cut the stems off; cut into thick slices, sprinkle with salt and drain in a colander to lose the excess water for about 1 hour. Dry with a kitchen paper towel, deep fry in the vegetable oil, then let drip.
Place a layer of eggplants in a baking-pan then layer some tomato sauce, some of the grated cheese, some leaves of basil and slices of primosale. Cover with other eggplants and continue in the same way until ingredients have finished. Top with the sauce and sprinkle abundantly with grated cheese and bake for about 30 minutes. Cool down and turn out on a course dish.

"Taboulè"

4 servings

10 ounces of precooked cuscus
1/2 red pepper
1/2 yellow pepper
2 lemons
2 firm red tomatoes
1 stalk of celery
3 ounces of tuna in oil
parsley, **1 tuft**
basil, **1 tuft**
mint, **1 tuft**
8 tbsp extra virgin olive oil
salt, pepper TT

Soften the cuscus in 1 1/2 cups of salted hot water and add 1 tbsp of oil.
Transfer to a tray and cool down. Mince the mint, the basil and the parsley and combine with oil, lemon juice and pepper. Beat with a fork.
Crumble the cold cuscus with your hands or with two forks; then transfer to a bowl and season with the sauce.
Add the diced peppers and the celery, dice, and remove seeds from the tomatoes and dice the tuna. Mix and allow to rest in the fridge for some time before serving.

Sardines "a linguata"

4 servings

1 3/4 pounds of fresh sardines
1 cup flour
1/2 cup extra virgin olive oil
9 tbsp white vinegar
salt TT

Scale the sardines, open in halves and remove bones and head. Wash well.
Put in a bowl and cover with vinegar and soak for 30 min. Drip dry them on paper towels, flour the fish and fry it in hot oil, add salt only at the end.

Tuna "carpaccio"

4 servings

1 pound of thin slices of fresh tuna
4 lemons
parsley, **1 tuft**
basil, **1 tuft**
mint, **1 tuft**
3 tbsp extra virgin olive oil
salt, pepper TT

Wash and dry the tuna. Put the slices in one layer on a serving dish and trickle with lemon juice and oil. Sprinkle with the minced herbs, a pinch of salt and a dash of pepper. Allow to marinade before serving.

Panelle (Flat Garbanzo bean loaves)

6-8 servings

1 pound garbanzo bean flour
2 cups vegetable oil
salt, pepper TT

Sift the flour in a saucepan and slowly add 6 cups of salted water, mixing with a wooden spoon, to avoid lumps. Set the saucepan on a low flame and let the mixture thicken stirring in the same direction for about 40 minutes.

By then the mixture should detach from the saucepan; add the minced parsley and turn the paste upside down in a non-stick rectangular baking-pan, sprinkled with cold water. Flatten the surface of the mixture and let it harden.

After the mixture has cooled down completely and hardened enough, turn it upside-down and slice thinly, giving the shape of triangles or other shapes, as pleased.

Fry the panelle in hot oil. Drain, sprinkle with salt and pepper and serve.

Sardines "a beccafico"

4 servings

- **1 3/4 pounds** of fresh sardines
- **5 ounces** of breadcrumbs
- **3 ounces** of fillets of anchovy in oil
- **1 tbsp** of pecorino (or Parmesan cheese), grated
- **1 1/3** ounces of raisins
- **1 1/3** ounces of pine nuts
- parsley, **1 tuft**
- **2** lemons
- **2** cloves of garlic
- **8 tbsp** extra virgin olive oil
- **10** bay leaves in halves
- salt, pepper TT

Scale the sardines, open in halves and remove bones and head. Wash well and allow to dry on kitchen paper towels. Brown the peeled and crushed garlic in a frying pan with the oil. Discard and leave the breadcrumbs to flavour. Turn off the flame and add the grated cheese, the anchovies melted in oil, the pine nuts, the raisins and the minced parsley. Stir in salt and pepper. Put on each sardine a pinch of salt and a little of the bread crumb mixture. Roll them up forming little roulades and stick them with wooden skewers, alternating the roulades with slices of lemon and bay leaves and put in a greasy baking-pan.

Trickle with oil and lemon juice and cook in the oven at 375° F, for about 15 minutes.

Dressed olives

4 servings

- **1 pound** of pickled green olives
- **3** cloves of garlic
- **2** carrots
- **1** stalk of celery
- parsley, 1 tuft
- **8 tbsp** extra virgin olive oil
- **3 tbsp** white vinegar
- **1/2** teaspoon oregano
- pepper TT

Crush the olives with the pestle of the mortar and put them in a bowl. Season them with minced garlic and parsley, a pinch of oregano and a mixture of oil, vinegar and pepper. Add the carrots and celery cut in sticks. Mix with care and let flavour for some time, before serving.

Peperonata
(peppers and potatoes)

4 servings

2 pounds of peppers
3 medium ripe tomatoes
1 1/3 pounds of potatoes
1 big onion
basil, 1 bu.
5 tbsp extra virgin olive oil
salt, pepper TT

Wash and dry the peppers, remove the seeds and cut into slices. Peel and slice the potatoes. Finely slice the onion and sauté in a saucepan with abundant extra virgin olive oil. Add the peppers and let marinate for 5 minutes. Add the potatoes, cover and cook for about ten minutes. Add the tomatoes, seedless, and chopped. Add the basil, a pinch of salt and a dash of pepper, and cook for about 20 minutes on moderate flame, stirring from time to time and adding a few spoons of warm water if the sauce reduced too much. Cool down before serving.

Eggplant roulades

4 servings

2 eggplants
7 ounces of breadcrumbs
8 fillets of anchovies in oil
2 tbsp of pecorino (or Parmesan cheese), grated
1 cup of tomato sauce
1 1/3 ounces of raisins
1 1/3 ounces of pine nuts
parsley, **1 tuft**
basil, **1 tuft**
1 cup extra virgin olive oil
salt, pepper TT

Wash and slice the eggplants; sprinkle with salt and put in a colander to drain the water in excess for about 1 hour. Put the breadcrumbs in a bowl. Smash the fillets of anchovy in little oil and add them to the breadcrumbs, the grated cheese, the raisins, the pine nuts, the minced herbs, a pinch of salt and a dash of pepper and mix well. Stir in a few tbsp of tomato sauce to thicken. Fry the eggplants in the hot extra virgin olive oil. Cover each slice with the prepared mixture. Roll them up and put in a greased baking-pan. Cook au gratin in warm oven for about ten minutes and serve with the tomato sauce aside.

Cauliflower Croquettes

4 servings

1 big cauliflower
1 egg
2 tbsp grated Parmesan cheese
1/2 cup flour
2 cups vegetable oil
salt, pepper TT

Cut off outer leaves and stalk and wash the cauliflower; boil in abundant salted water and drain carefully. Mash with a fork and put the purée in a bowl. Add a handful of Parmesan cheese, a beaten egg and sprinkle with pepper.
Add enough flour to make the mix soft. Take a spoonful of the mixture at a time, shape into croquettes and coat with flour. Deep fry in abundant hot oil; drain and put on a dish with paper towels.
Serve hot or warm.

Cauliflowers in batter

4 servings

1 medium cauliflower
7 ounces flour
1/3 ounces brewer's yeast
1 cup extra virgin olive oil
salt TT

Sieve the flour in a bowl and add yeast dissolved in little lukewarm water. Add water to make a creamy batter. Add a pinch of salt and let leaven for about 1 hour. Husk the cauliflower; cut off outer leaves and stalk and boil in salted hot water. Drain al dente and cool down. Dip the cauliflower tops in the batter and fry in hot oil. Drip and serve.

Eggplant "Caponata"

4 servings

4 medium eggplants
3 1/2 ounces of pit green olives
1 tbsp of pine nuts
1 tbsp of raisins
1 tbsp of capers
1 stalk of celery with leaves
1 cup of tomato sauce
1/2 onion
basil
5 tbsp extra virgin olive oil
5 tbsp vinegar
1 tbsp sugar
2 cups vegetable oil
salt, pepper TT

Stuffed peppers

4 servings

4 peppers
7 ounces of bread-
crumbs
1/2 onion
6 fillets of anchovy in
oil
1 clove of garlic
parsley, **1 tuft**
1 tbsp of pine nuts
1 tbsp of raisins
1 tbsp of grated pe-
corino cheese
7 tbsp extra virgin
olive oil
salt, pepper TT

Wash and dice the eggplants; sprinkle with salt and leave for about 1 hour in a colander to drain the excess water. Dry carefully then deep fry in seed oil. When golden, drain and put on kitchen paper towels. Husk and chop the celery and sauté in a frying pan with olive oil and the sliced onion. Add the pine nuts, the raisins, the capers, the olives and 1 minute after the tomato sauce. Add salt, pepper and the minced basil leaves and simmer for about 10 minutes. Stir in the vinegar sweetened with 1 tbsp of sugar, and allow to evaporate a little. Combine the eggplants; mix and turn the flame off. Transfer the "caponata" on a course dish and cool down before serving.

Wash the peppers and dry them. Grill and peel them, remove stem ends, seeds and cut them in pieces. Grease the inside of a baking pan with oil and cover with 2/3 of the peppers and keep aside. Mince the onion and brown in a frying pan with the oil. Add the chopped fillets of anchovy and dissolve them in the seasoning; add the breadcrumbs, mix and turn off the flame. Combine the grated pecorino, the pine nuts, the raisins (softened in lukewarm water and squeezed) and the minced garlic and parsley. Season with a pinch of salt and a dash of pepper and transfer to the baking-pan with the peppers. Cover with the remaining pieces of peppers; trickle with oil and cook in the oven at 375° F for about 30 minutes. Cool down before turning out on a course dish.

Stuffed artichokes

4 servings

8 artichokes
5 ounces of breadcrumbs
parsley, **1 tuft**
2 cloves of garlic
6 fillets of anchovy in oil
1 tbsp of pecorino (or Parmesan cheese), grated
2 lemons
1/2 cup extra virgin olive oil
salt, pepper TT

Snip off sharp leaf tips of the artichokes and the harder external leaves; scoop out the fuzzy chokes. Soak in water and lemon juice, to prevent blackening.

Put the breadcrumbs in a bowl; add the minced garlic, the parsley and the fillets of anchovy mashed in little oil, the grated cheese, a pinch of salt and a dash of black pepper.

Soften the mixture with oil and put in the artichoke hearts, well drained and salted.

Arrange the vegetables upright in a saucepan and pour inside some water and oil. Cover and cook for 30 minutes on moderate flame.

Fish croquettes

4 servings

1 1/2 pounds of whitebait
2 eggs
1 tbsp of grated Parmesan cheese
2 tbsp flour
parsley, **1 tuft**
6 tbsp extra virgin olive oil
salt, pepper TT

Beat the eggs in a bowl with a pinch of salt. Add flour, the Parmesan cheese, a dash of pepper and the minced parsley and mix well. Stir in the whitebait and let rest for a few minutes. Drop a tbsp of the mixture in a frying pan with abundant oil to obtain croquettes.

Turn over once and serve warm.

Cauliflower stew

4 servings

1 cauliflower
1 1/2 cups chopped tomatoes
2 ounces raisins and pine nuts
1 medium onion
parsley, **1 tuft**
8 tbsp dry white wine
5 tbsp extra virgin olive oil
salt, pepper TT

Chop and brown the onion in a saucepan with the oil, the raisins and the pine nuts, add the tomato and let flavor. Add the cauliflower tops and the minced parsley and cook on medium heat for about 20 minutes. Add the wine, a pinch of salt and a dash of pepper and cook for another 25 minutes.

"Matarocco" sauce on toast

4 servings

8 ripe tomatoes
4 cloves of garlic
basil, **1/2 bu.**
8 slices of toasted homemade bread
8 tbsp extra virgin olive oil
salt, pepper TT

Wash the tomatoes and blanch them for 5 minutes. Peel, remove seeds and chop them. Put the leaves of basil in a mortar with the garlic and a pinch of salt and crush for a long time; add some of the tomatoes and a trickle of oil and you keep crushing to obtain a thick cream. Put the mixture in a bowl and add 1/2 glass of oil and the remaining diced tomatoes. Season with a dash of black pepper and serve on the toasts.

BREADS
AND PIZZAS

Breads and pizzas, of the wood-burning oven, always bring so much joy to the table. A smoking loaf of bread seasoned with cheese, tomato and anchovies easily draws pleasant company, friends and family. As do the flat breads and "rianate" pizzas. Breads and pizzas, most derived from the poor farmers have in time become gourmet treats. Today young people have learned to appreciate the wood-burning oven which guarantees the best results to these traditional delights.

Bread "cunzato"

4 servings

1 loaf of homemade bread of about 1 pound
4 big ripe tomatoes
3 1/2 ounces of fillets of anchovy in oil
5 ounces of cheese primosale
(or mozzarella) in slices
1/2 cup extra virgin olive oil
1/2 teaspoon oregano
salt, pepper TT

Cut the loaf of bread lengthwise while still warm (or heat in oven); make slits in the crust on each half and sprinkle with salt, pepper, oregano and add the oil.

Layer tomatoes, thin slices of cheese, the chopped fillets of anchovy on one half.

Sprinkle with more oregano. Cover with the other half and slightly press the crust.

"Sfincione"

4 servings

1 3/4 pounds flour
1 ounce brewer's yeast
2 onions
1 pound of peeled tomatoes
3 1/2 ounces of sliced fresh caciocavallo
(substitute American style mozzarella)
3 1/2 ounces of fillets of anchovy in oil
1 teaspoon oregano
1/2 cup bread crumbs
1/3 cup extra virgin olive oil
salt, pepper TT

Combine flour and yeast, dissolved in warm water, to make a smooth dough. Put dough in a floured bowl; cover and let rest for a couple of hours.

In the meantime chop the onions and sauté in a saucepan with some oil and a few tablespoons of water.

Stir in the chopped tomatoes, a pinch of salt and pepper and cook for about twenty minutes.

Roll out the dough into a round about 1 1/4 in. thick. Put in a greased baking-pan.

Top with bits of anchovy, slightly sticking them to the pizza.

Sprinkle the grated cheese and cover with sauce.

Sprinkle with oregano and bread crumbs.

Bake at 425 F. for 20 minutes.

"Rianata" (pizza)

4 servings

1 1/2 pounds flour
3/4 ounces of brewer's yeast
4 medium ripe tomatoes
8 cloves of garlic
3 1/2 ounces of grated pecorino
parsley, **1 tuft**
3 1/2 ounces of fillets of anchovy in oil
1 teaspoon oregano
salt TT

Dissolve the yeast in warm water and combine with flour. Knead vigorously adding salted warm water to make a moderately stiff dough, smooth and elastic.

Shape into a ball and put in a floured bowl. Cover with a cloth and let rise for about 2 hours. Knead quickly and divide dough in small balls.

Roll out the dough into a thin round on a slightly greased baking-pan.

Chop the anchovies and spread over round.

Chop the tomatoes and mix with the chopped garlic and parsley; spread on the pizza.

Top with the grated pecorino, the oregano and trickle some oil.

Bake at 485 F. for about 20 minutes.

"Cabbucio" (sandwich)

4 servings

1 1/2 pound of home made leavened
dough for bread
8 big ripe tomatoes
7 ounces of sliced salami
1 pound of mozzarella
1/2 teaspoon oregano
5 tbsp extra virgin olive oil
salt TT

Trickle some oil on the dough and knead energetically for a few minutes. Divide dough in 4 loaves.

Punch down and put a greased baking-pan; let rest for 15-20 minutes.

Grease the surface of loaves with a little oil and bake in a hot oven. When the "cabbucis" are brown, take out from the oven and cut the loaves lengthwise. Layer the sliced tomatoes and the sliced mozzarella on one half. Sprinkle salt and oregano and top with salami. Cover with the other half and put the loaves back in the oven to make the cheese melt. Eat warm.

SALADS

Fresh salads are sometimes a valid alternative to a meal. Color and spice joyfully combine different textures and tastes.
Salt, extra virgin olive oil, pepper and oranges give "simple" ingredients new life.
Snails with garlic and mint; seasoned octopus; tomatoes, garlic and basil "salamoreci", evoke ancient times.

Snail salad

4 servings

2 pounds of snails
3 cloves of garlic
some parsley
some mint leaves
5 tbsp extra virgin olive oil
salt, pepper TT

Wash the snails carefully; then boil them for 15 minutes, skimming, if necessary, with a slotted spoon. Drain the snails and rinse them; put them back in the saucepan with clean water, moderately salted and cook for another 15 minutes.
In the meantime, cut the garlic and put it in a small bowl. Add the parsley and mint, minced, and mix with abundant oil. Flavour with a pinch of salt and pepper and beat with a fork. Drain the snails and transfer to a course dish. Season with the prepared sauce and let flavour for a few minutes before serving.

Octopus salad

4 servings

2 pounds of octopus
2 cloves of garlic
2 stalks of celery
4 carrots
parsley, **1/4 bu.**
1/3 teaspoon oregano
5 tbsp extra virgin olive oil
2 tbsp white vinegar
salt, pepper TT

Boil the octopus in salted hot water; turn off the gas and cool down.
Drain and separate the head (that you can serve apart) from the tentacles. Cut these to pieces. Transfer to a serving dish, add the celery in disks and slice the carrots.
Mince the garlic and parsley and put in a bowl. Add a glass of oil, a trickle of vinegar, a pinch of oregano, one of salt and a dash of pepper. Mix well. Add to salad and let flavour for a few minutes before serving.

"Pantesca" salad

4 servings

- **4** medium potatoes
- **3** tomatoes
- **1** red onion, sliced in rings
- **2** spoons of salted capers
- **5 ounces** green olives
- **7 ounces** of mackerels in oil
- **5 tbsp** extra virgin olive oil
- **1/2 tbsp** oregano
- salt, pepper TT

Wash the potatoes and boil them in slightly salted water. Drain and cool. Peel and cut to pieces and transfer to a course dish.
Wash the tomatoes and split in halves. Remove seeds. Slice and add to the potatoes.
Add the olives and the onion rings. Remove salt from capers, drip and chop the mackerels and add to the rest. Season the salad with oil, oregano, salt and pepper and serve.

Orange salad

4 servings

- **4** oranges
- **3 tbsp** extra virgin olive oil
- salt, pepper TT

Peel the oranges and strip off the skin from every segment; put on a serving dish.
Trickle some oil in a bowl, add a pinch of salt, dust abundantly with pepper and beat with a fork. Season the fruit with this dressing and let rest a few minutes before serving.

"Salamureci" (tomato salad)

4 servings

2 pounds of mature tomatoes
3 cloves of garlic
5 large leaves of basil, minced
4 tbsp extra virgin olive oil
1 cup diced stale homemade bread
salt, pepper TT

Chop the tomatoes, put them in a bowl and
sprinkle with the minced basil, some oil,
salt and pepper. Let flavour for a few minutes;
then cover with cold water and add the diced
stale bread. Serve immediately.

Turkish salad

Per 4 persone

3 medium potatoes
2 onions
1 medium eggplant
1 red pepper
1 yellow pepper
3 cloves of garlic
1/2 teaspoon oregano
5 tbsp extra virgin olive oil
1 tbsp vinegar
salt, pepper TT

Wash and dry the peppers. Grill, peel and slice
them.
Wash the eggplants and cut off the stalk. Peel the
potatoes and the onions. Slice all the vegetables
and cook on a hot grill.
Transfer all the vegetables on a course dish; season
them with minced garlic, oil, vinegar, oregano, salt
and pepper.

SOUPS

*These recipes belong almost
exclusively to an oral tradition,
many passed on from mother to
daughter over hundreds of years.
They reveal the very strong
character of the culture from
which they originate. Bound to
the succession of seasons in the
countryside and to the type of fish
caught along the coasts, these
dishes are often characteristic of
parties and religious
celebrations. Some are made of
inexpensive ingredients, but all
are nourishing, tasty and
popular. Flavored with plenty of
extra virgin olive oil, they are
almost always accompanied by
stale bread.*

Ricotta raviolis in broth

4 servings

> **2 1/2** cups of durum wheat flour
> **1 pound** of fresh sheep ricotta
> **5 tbsp** grated Parmesan cheese
> **6** cups of chicken broth
> parsley, 1 tuft
> salt, pepper TT

Sift the flour with a pinch of salt and make a well. Add a little warm water and knead well for about 15 minutes to make a smooth and moderately stiff dough. Make a roll, fold and let rest under an upside-down bowl for 1 hour. In the meantime, sieve the ricotta and season with a pinch of salt and a dash of pepper; add the grated cheese, some minced parsley and mix well. Roll out the dough in thin sheets on a floured surface. With a spoon, distribute dollops of the mixture at regular distance one from the other. Fold the filling inside and seal with fingers. With a pastry cutter cut them out into crescent-shapes, Boil the skimmed chicken broth and add the "cassatelle" . Serve with the hot broth, some minced parsley and, separately, some grated cheese.

"Tenerumi" soup and "Picchi-pacchi" sauce

4 servings

> **2 pounds** of "tenerumi" (leaves and buds of long zucchini)
> **4** big ripe tomatoes
> **2** cloves of garlic
> **1** medium onion
> basil, 1 tuft
> **2** cups of cut spaghetti (or linguine)
> **3 tbsp** extra virgin olive oil
> salt, pepper TT

Husk the "tenerumi", eliminating the hardest leaves; wash carefully. Drain and chop them. Boil in abundant salted water.
In the meantime, peel the tomatoes, remove the seeds and chop them.
Mince and sauté the onion in a frying pan with some oil and the clove of garlic. Add the chopped tomatoes, the salt, pepper and the basil and simmer for 15 minutes.
When the vegetables are cooked, add the pasta and cook on moderate flame, stirring frequently. At the end add the sauce to the soup and let rest a few minutes before serving.

Pasta with potatoes

4 servings

2 pounds of potatoes
2 cups of short pasta
8 cups of meat broth
1 onion
parsley, **1 tuft**
3 tbsp extra virgin olive oil
salt, pepper TT

Sauté the minced onion, in a saucepan, with a little oil. Stir in the potatoes, peeled and diced, and brown for a couple of minutes, stirring. Season with ground black pepper and cover with the warm broth. Cook on moderate flame for about 40 minutes. Add salt and the pasta and cook al dente, stirring from time to time. At the end season with the minced parsley. Serve warm.

Zucchini and potato soup

4 servings

1 long zucchini
1 pound potatoes
2 cups short pasta
1 onion
1 stalk of celery
4 ripe tomatoes
5 tbsp extra virgin olive oil
salt, pepper TT

Peel and dice the zucchini and the potatoes. Finely chop the onion and the stalk of celery and sauté in a saucepan, with little oil. Add the peeled, seedless and chopped tomatoes, and let flavour for a couple of minutes, stirring from time to time. Stir in the diced vegetables and cover with a little warm water. Add salt and cook for about 40 minutes. Add 4 cups of warm water and boil. Add salt TT and stir in the pasta. At the end season the soup with a dash of ground black pepper and a trickle of oil. Serve warm.

"St. Joseph's" soup

4 servings

7 ounces of dried kidney beans
7 ounces of lentils
1 pound of assorted vegetables
(cauliflower, potatoes, carrots, etc.)
1 bunch of wild fennel
2 cups of short pasta
2 tbsp extra virgin olive oil
salt TT

Soak the legumes for one night.
Drain and rinse them. Put them in a saucepan and cover with abundant water. Add salt and cook for 1 hour. Clean, dice and boil the vegetables in salted water. When cooked, drain and transfer to the casserole with the beans and lentils; cook for another 20 minutes. Add hot water if necessary. Add the pasta and cook al dente on moderate flame, stirring from time to time. Season the soup with a trickle of oil.

"Frascatole" with cauliflower

4 servings

2 1/2 cups of durum wheat semolina
1 cauliflower
3 1/2 ounces bacon
4 tbsp extra virgin olive oil
salt, pepper TT

Sift the semola in a bowl and thicken with a circular motion adding spoonfuls of salted water and making grains as big as lentils. Transfer the frascatole on a clean cloth, cover and let rest for a couple of hours. Husk the cauliflower and cut it into sprouts. Brown the bacon and crumble it in a saucepan, with a little oil; add abundant salted water and boil. Add the sprouts and cook for 15 minutes. Add the frascatoles and cook, stirring, for about 1 hour. Season with a trickle of oil and a dash of pepper. Let rest for a few minutes before serving.

"Maccu" with croutons

4 servings

> **2 pounds** of fresh, shelled broad beans
> **3** slices of homemade bread
> **4 tbsp** extra virgin olive oil
> salt, pepper TT

Peel the broad beans and put in a saucepan. Cover with cold salted water and cook for a couple of hours, stirring frequently and crushing them with a wooden spatula.

When the soup has become a thick purée, season with a dash of pepper and a trickle of oil.

Cool down and serve with some dices of bread, fried with little oil.

Fish soup

4 servings

> **1 pound** of fish for soup
> **2** cups of cut spaghetti (or other type of short pasta)
> **1 pound** of ripe tomatoes
> **2** cloves of garlic
> **1** onion
> **1** bay leaf
> parsley, **1 tuft**
> **1 tbsp** of peeled almonds
> **3 tbsp** extra virgin olive oil
> Cayenne pepper TT
> salt TT

Clean the fish; sprinkle with salt and put aside. Finely chop the onion and brown in a saucepan with the bay leaf (that you will eliminate) and a trickle of oil. Add the peeled, seedless and chopped tomatoes and let flavour for a few minutes, stirring from time to time. Season with a pinch of Cayenne pepper, cover with abundant warm water and boil. Add the garlic, parsley and almonds, minced; mix and boil the fish in the prepared broth. When cooked, transfer to a dish. Filter, with a tight-meshed strainer, the liquid and pour it in another casserole. Clean the fish, eliminating all the bones and put the chopped pulp in the casserole with the broth. Add salt TT and boil. Cook the pasta in the soup and serve warm, after sprinkling with some minced parsley.

"Sciusceddu"
(veal and ricotta soup)

4 servings

- **9 ounces** of ground veal
- **1 pound** of ricotta cheese
- **3** cups of chicken broth
- **5** eggs
- parsley, **1 tuft**
- grated Parmesan cheese, **1 tbsp**
- dried breadcrumbs, **1/4** cup
- salt, pepper TT

Put the minced veal in a bowl and mix with an egg, 1 tbsp of grated Parmesan cheese, some minced parsley, salt, pepper and the breadcrumbs. Mix to obtain a stiff and homogeneous dough. Make balls as big as olives and put in a pot with the boiling broth. Separate the yolks from the egg whites and whisk the egg whites until stiff. Mix the yolks with the ricotta, the minced parsley, a handful of grated Parmesan, and a pinch of salt and pepper. Transfer the broth and rissoles to a baking-pan, preferably oven proof earthenware; add the egg whites to the mixture of eggs and ricotta. Spread over veal mixture and cover completely. Bake in warm oven for about ten minutes and serve immediately.

"Frittedda"
(vegetable soup)

4 servings

- **2 pounds** of fresh broad beans
- **1 1/2 pounds** of fresh peas
- **4** artichokes
- **1** onion
- **1** lemon
- **5 tbsp** extra virgin olive oil
- parsley, **1 tuft**
- salt, pepper TT

Shell the broad beans and the peas; wash and drain them. Remove the harder external leaves of the artichokes. Cut the tips off, cut the artichokes in segments and soak in water with lemon juice. Finely chop the onion and brown it in a saucepan with the oil. Drain the artichokes, add them to the onion and let flavour for a couple of minutes; then add the broad beans and the peas. Add 1 cup of warm water, salt, pepper and some minced parsley. Cook with lid on a low flame, for 25-30 minutes.

Garbanzo beans and rice soup

4 servings

1 1/4 pounds garbanzo beans
1 1/2 cups of rice
1 onion
5 tbsp extra virgin olive oil
1/16 tbsp baking soda
salt, pepper TT

Soak the garbanzo beans with a pinch of baking soda for over night. Chop and brown the onion in a saucepan with 3 tbsp of oil. Add the garbanzo beans and season with a pinch of salt and a dash of pepper. Cover with water and cook for a couple of hours. Stir in the raw rice and let cook.
Drizzle the top with a little extra virgin olive oil.

Snails "A' Ghiotta"

4 servings

2 pounds of clean snails
1 1/2 pounds of potatoes
4 ripe tomatoes
1 onion
parsley, **1 tuft**
3 tbsp extra virgin olive oil
salt, pepper TT

Clean the snails, then boil them for 15 minutes, skimming, if necessary, with a slotted spoon. Drain the snails; rinse them and boil them for another 15 minutes in clean water.
In the meantime, sauté some minced onion and parsley in a saucepan with a little oil; add the peeled, seedless and chopped tomatoes and let flavour, stirring, for a couple of minutes. Brown the peeled and diced potatoes in the sauce, then cover with 4 cups of water. Add salt, pepper and cook, with the lid, on moderate flame, for about twenty minutes.
At the end of the second boiling, rinse the snails again and drain them; add them to the soup and keep cooking for another 10 minutes. Let rest for a few minutes before serving.

FIRST COURSES

The supremacy of pasta on the island is ancient. Some historians suggest macaroni was conceived here for the first time. Pasta is present in the diet of Sicilians at least once a day; sometimes it is the only course. Long, short, fresh or dried it is accompanied by all the products of the island. Basic in the Sicilian diet, pasta is always rich in different ingredients. In the countryside and along the coasts. So every town has its pasta seasoning using local ingredients. Grandmothers' recipes become a discriminating factor even between families, according to tradition established in time.

Swordfish & Eggplant pasta

4 servings

1 pound pasta "busiate" (twisted homemade spaghetti)
1 pound peeled tomatoes, chopped
10 ounces of sliced of swordfish
1 clove of garlic
1 eggplant
1 medium onion
basil, **1 tuft**
fresh mint, **1 tuft**
1 tbsp of blanched almonds
3 tbsp dry white wine
1 cup extra virgin olive oil
salt, pepper TT

Chop the onion and brown it in a saucepan, with a little oil. Add the chopped tomatoes, the basil, a pinch of salt and pepper and cook for 20 minutes, on moderate flame, add water if necessary. Wash and dice the eggplant, sprinkle with salt and drain the water in excess in a colander for 1 hour. Rinse, dry and brown in hot oil. Skin and dice the swordfish and sprinkle with a little salt. Then brown in a saucepan for a minute with a drizzle of oil and a clove of garlic. Sprinkle with wine and let evaporate. Remove the garlic and transfer the fish to the saucepan with the tomato sauce. Cook on moderate flame for another ten minutes. Boil the pasta in salty hot water; strain "al dente" and toss in the saucepan with the fish sauce. Add the eggplants, the minced almonds and the minced mint. Mix well and serve.

Pasta "alla Norma"

4 servings

1 pound of long pasta (hollow spaghetti)
1 medium eggplant
3 1/2 ounces of salted ricotta
2 pounds of ripe tomatoes
2 cloves of garlic
basil, **1 tuft**
1 cup extra virgin olive oil
salt, pepper TT

Cut a small "X" at the base the tomatoes.
Blanch them for about ten minutes.
Peel, remove seeds and chop.
Brown the cloves of garlic in a saucepan with a little oil. Remove the garlic.
Add the tomatoes, the leaves of basil, a dash of salt and pepper.
Mix and simmer to thicken.
Dice the eggplant put in a colander and sprinkle with salt for about 1 hour.
Brown in hot oil. Cook the pasta in salted boiling water drain at "al dente" and transfer to saucepan with the tomato sauce.
Mix and add the eggplants, a handful of fresh basil leaves and the grated salted ricotta.

Pasta with sardines

4 servings

- **1 pound** of pasta bucatini (hollow spaghetti)
- **1 1/2 pounds** of sardines
- **1 pound** of farmer fennel
- **1** small bag of saffron
- **1** onion
- **2 tb.** of pine nuts
- **2 tb.** of raisins
- **3 salted** anchovies (or 3 1/2 ounces of fillets of anchovy in oil)
- **5 tbsp** extra virgin olive oil
- **3 tbsp** dry white wine
- salt, pepper TT

Bone, rinse and flake the sardines.

Clean the fennels removing the hardest parts and boil in salted water. Drain, but retain the water. Chop the fennel finely.

Brown a shredded onion in a saucepan with a half cup of oil.

Add the anchovies and dissolve in the seasoning. Add the pine nuts, the fennel, the raisins and the sardines and let flavour, stirring well. Sprinkle with some wine and let evaporate; dissolve the saffron in a cup of the vegetable broth. Add salt and pepper and cook for about 20 minutes.

Cook the pasta al dente in the fennel water.

Mix with the sauce and let rest for about ten minutes before serving.

Trapani's pesto & pasta

4 servings

- **1 pound** pasta "busiate" (twisted homemade spaghetti)
- **2 pounds** of ripe tomatoes
- **4 cloves** of garlic
- **3 1/2 ounces** peeled and toasted almonds basil, **1 tuft**
- **1/2** cup extra virgin olive oil
- **4 tbsp** grated pecorino (or Parmesan cheese)
- salt, pepper TT

Blanch for 5 minutes, peel, remove seeds and chop the tomatoes. Crush the almonds with a pinch of salt for a

long time in a mortar (or a food processor). Transfer to a bowl and put the garlic, some basil and a pinch of salt in the mortar and crush. Add the tomatoes and continue crushing until well combined. Transfer to the bowl with the crushed almonds and stir in the oil, salt TT and a plentiful dusting of black pepper. Mix and let rest for a couple of hours. Cook the pasta in salted water, drain al dente and season with the sauce. Serve the grated pecorino (or Parmesan) on the side.

Spaghetti with sea urchins

4 servings

1 pound of spaghetti
40 sea urchins (eggs can be found in some Asian food stores)
2 cloves of garlic
parsley, **1 tuft**
5 tbsp extra virgin olive oil
1 piece Cayenne pepper
salt TT

Carefully open the sea urchins with the special utensil or a pair of scissors and scoop the eggs out putting them in a bowl. Peel the garlic, crush and brown it in a frying pan with a cup of oil, the minced parsley and a bit of crushed Cayenne pepper. Let rest for the time needed to cook the pasta. Boil the spaghetti "al dente" in salted hot water. Drain and season with the sauce. Top with the sea urchin eggs and serve.

Tuna sauce and pasta

4 servings

1 pound pasta "busiate" (twisted homemade spaghetti)
a single slice of fresh tuna of 1 pound
2 cloves of garlic
mint, **1** handfull
1 onion
9 ounces of shelled peas
1 bay leaf
3 cups of tomato concentrate
7 tbsp extra virgin olive oil
8 tbsp dry white wine
1/3 teaspoon sugar
salt, pepper TT

Soak the tuna in cold water for 30 minutes; dry and score by making shallow diagonal cuts 1 inch apart. Insert the garlic and mint, minced, in the cuts.
Brown 1/2 chopped onion in a saucepan with the oil and stir in the peas. Add the tomato concentrate and season with salt, pepper and a pinch of sugar. Mix and simmer to thicken for 15 minutes.
Brown the bay leaf and the remaining onion in 4 spoons of oil in a frying pan; add the tuna and brown. Wet with the wine and let evaporate; transfer the fish to the casserole with the sauce. Add 1 cup of warm water and cook for about 40 minutes.
Cook the pasta in salted water and drain al dente. Season with the sauce and the bits of tuna.

Baked ring pasta

4 servings

- **14 ounces** of ring pasta
- **9 ounces** of minced veal
- **7 ounces** of shelled peas
- **3** cups of tomato sauce
- **1/2** onion
- **1/2** carrot
- **1** stalk of celery
- fresh parsley
- fresh basil
- **2 ounces** of grated caciocavallo
- **5 tbsp** dry white wine
- **2 tbsp** extra virgin olive oil
- **1 ounces** butter
- **4 tbsp** bread crumbs
- sugar TT
- salt and pepper TT

Brown the minced onion, carrot, celery and parsley with 1 tablespoon of extra virgin olive oil and a little of butter. Add the minced meat and cook on a low flame, then add some wine and let it evaporate. Add the peas and simmer; then pour in the tomato sauce and add some salt, pepper, basil and a little of sugar. Stir and simmer for 40 minutes, adding some warm water, if the sauce reduces too much. Cook the pasta "al dente" in boiling salty water. Drain, season with the ragù sauce and the grated caciocavallo (leave 1 tablespoon). Pour the seasoned pasta in a buttered baking-pan sprinkled with bread crumbs. Over the top sprinkle with the bread crumbs and the remaining cheese. Then bake at 392° F for about 40 minutes. Instead of the baking-pan use 4 little molds to reduce the baking time to 15-20 minutes.

Spaghetti with fried zucchini and mint

4 servings

- **14 ounces** of spaghetti
- **4** medium zucchini
- **2** cloves of garlic
- fresh mint, tuft
- **1/2** cup extra virgin olive oil
- **1** small pepper
- salt TT

Wash and dry the zucchini; slice and season with salt. Chop the garlic and brown in a pan with a cup of oil and the pepper in pieces. Remove garlic from oil, fry the sliced zucchini and drain. Cook the spaghetti "al dente" in plenty of boiling salty water. Drain the pasta and pour it in the pan with the oil in which you have already fried the zucchini. Add the zucchini, stir. Garnish with the mint and serve.

Spaghetti with bread crumbs and anchovies

4 servings

14 ounces of spaghetti
1/2 cup of bread crumbs
5 salted anchovies
2 cloves of garlic
1/2 cup extra virgin olive oil
salt TT

Remove salt from the anchovies and fillet them. Brown the bread crumbs with some oil. Brown the garlic in a saucepan with plenty of extra virgin olive oil. Remove the garlic and dissolve the anchovies in the oil to obtain a smooth sauce. Add 3 tablespoons of cooking water of the pasta, season with pepper and switch off the flame. Cook the spaghetti "al dente" in plenty of salted water. drain; season the pasta with the prepared sauce. Top with the toasted bread crumbs.

Pasta with cauliflowers

4 servings

1 pound Bucatini: [boo-kah-TEE-nee] Hollow, spaghetti.
1 medium cauliflower
2 ounces large golden raisins
1 ounce of pine nuts
1 small bag of saffron
2 ounces fillets of anchovy in oil
5 tbsp extra virgin olive oil
salt, pepper TT

Cut off tops, the florets, of cauliflower and parboil in salted water for 5 minutes.
Drain and put aside the cooking water.
Brown the minced onion in a saucepan with plenty of oil.
Add the fillets of anchovy drained and chopped and dissolve in the oil.
Add the raisins, the pine nuts and the cauliflower and brown on moderate flame, stirring often.
Dissolve the saffron in 1/2 cup of cauliflower broth.
Add salt, pepper TT and cook for 15 minutes.
Cook the bucatini "al dente" in the remaining broth. Drain and stir them into the saucepan with the sauce.
Let rest for one minute before serving

Lasagna with meat sauce and ricotta cheese

4 servings

- **1 pound** of lasagna
- **7 ounces** of minced veal
- **7 ounces** of pork sausage
- **1** onion
- **4 cups** of tomato sauce
- **14 ounces** of sheep ricotta cheese
fresh parsley
- **5 tbsp** red wine
- **5 tbsp** grated pecorino cheese
- **2 tbsp** extra virgin olive oil
- **1 ounces** butter
salt and pepper TT

Brown the minced onion in a saucepan with a drizzle of oil and a daub of butter. Add the minced meat and the skinned sausage and cook all together at low heat. Add the wine and let evaporate. Then add the minced parsley with the tomato sauce. Season with salt and pepper and simmer for one hour, stirring occasionally. Add a little warm water keeping the sauce liquid. Boil the lasagna for about one minute in plenty of slightly salted water. Place them in cool water to stop the cooking. Dry on a cloth. When the ragù (meat sauce) sauce is ready, butter a baking-pan and put a sheet of pasta then pour on the pasta 4-5 tablespoons of ragù and sprinkle with some ricotta cheese. Sprinkle with some pecorino cheese and go on seasoning layer after layer till exhausting the ingredients. Bake the lasagna at 350° F. for about 1\2 hour. Cool for 10 minutes before serving.

Spaghetti with tuna botargo

4 servings

- **1 pound** of spaghetti
- **3 1/2 ounces** tuna botargo (dried and salted tuna eggs)
- **3** cloves of garlic
parsley, **2 tufts**
- **6 tbsp** extra virgin olive oil
- **1** small pepper, chopped
salt TT

Grate the tuna botargo and put aside in a bowl. Slice the garlic, add the cayenne pepper and the parsley minced, sauté in a frying pan with oil and 2 tablespoons of water. Cool down and add 2 tablespoons of tuna botargo. Cook the spaghetti "al dente" in salted hot water and drain. Season with the sauce and sprinkle with the remaining botargo. Garnish with a handful of minced parsley.

Couscous with fish

4 servings

- **1 pound** of semolina of durum wheat
- **2 pounds** of assorted fish for soup
- **1 pound** of ripe tomatoes
- **5** cloves of garlic
- **1** big onion
- fresh parsley
- **1 pound** of blanched almonds
- **1 pound** of mussels - steamed open with broth
- **2 pounds** of prawns
- **1 pound** of scorpion fish
- **1 pound** of bogues (typical Mediterranean fish) - filleted and boiled
- **1** cup flour
- **4** bay leaves
- **1/2** cup extra virgin olive oil
- Cayenne pepper TT
- salt and pepper TT

Sprinkle the semolina in the "mafaradda" (terra-cotta bowl with flared sides) with a little salty water and knead ("incocciatela") with a slow and circular movement.

Put the grains of couscous on a clean cloth and then let them dry up for a couple of hours.

Pour the couscous again in the "mafaradda" and add 1/2 cup of oil, coat well. Season with some parsley, 2 cloves of garlic and 1/2 onion all minced together, then sprinkle some Cayenne pepper.

Pour the seasoned semolina in the "cuscusiera" (special saucepan of earthenware with holes, replaceable with a colander of the same diameter of the pot on which it must be fitted), in which you have to put the bay leaves covering the holes. Put this special colander on a saucepan half filled of water and seal the edges of the two containers, wrapping around a cloth previously dampened and rubbed in flour where the containers meet to prevent the dispersion of steam. Cook for about 1 hour.

Mince the onion and brown it with oil, a bay leaf and some Cayenne pepper; add one peeled, chopped tomato and stir-fry. Cover with three cups of water, add salt and boil.

Add a mixture of minced garlic and almonds to the broth.

Add the fish, already cleaned and salted.

Cover the saucepan and cook at law heat for 25-30 minutes, in order to make the fish flake, thickening the soup.

Switch off the flame and let rest for 1\2 hour; then strain the broth from the soup.

Transfer the cooked couscous in the "mafaradda" and pour a cup of the broth on top.

Stir to absorb the broth and let rest for at least a couple of hours, under a woollen blanket. Boil the remaining broth and add the prawns, the mussels, the scorpion fishes and the prepared bogues.

Serve the cuscus with the fish and the broth on the side.

FISH

The origin of fishing along the Sicilian coastlines is lost in the mists of times. Archestrato, Greek poet of the 4th cen. B.C., writes of the pleasant taste of roasted tuna flavored with "salmoriglio" (fish sauce). Mackerels, swordfish, tuna and dried cod, cooked in a thousand ways are a pleasure for the palate. These fish are sometimes prepared in the same way in which meat is cooked: stuffed, grilled with sauces. Endless is the number of recipes with swordfish along the shores in Messina. Also true with tuna in western Sicily. Every single part of tuna, also called "pig of the sea", is used; even the bowels become a delicious spicy sausage which is eaten sliced and seasoned with olive oil.

Swordfish roulades

4 servings

12 thin slices of swordfish
5 ounces of breadcrumbs
1 ounce of pine nuts
2 ounes of raisins
fresh parsley
1 clove of garlic
2 tablespoons of grated pecorino cheese
2 lemons
6 bay leaves
1/2 cup extra virgin olive oil
salt and pepper TT

Mix the breadcrumbs with the pecorino cheese, the pine nuts, the raisins, the minced garlic and parsley, salt and pepper. Soften with oil and spread on the salted slices of fish.

Make roulades and close with a toothpick (that you will take out at the end of cooking); then put the roulades on a bed of lemon slices in an oiled baking-pan and sprinkle with bay leaves. Add a mixture of oil and lemon and bake at 350° F for 20 minutes.

Tuna with onion stew

4 servings

4 slices of fresh tuna fish
2 big onions
1 cup flour
8 tbsp extra virgin olive oil
8 tbsp white vinnegar
salt and pepper TT

Peel and slice the onions; brown them with 5 tablespoons of oil and 1/2 cup of water.
Add 1/2 cup of vinegar, season with salt and pepper and let evaporate.
Switch off the flame and pour the onion stew on a dish. Wash and dry up the tuna, add flour and salt and then fry in a pan with a little oil.
Transfer the fish in the dish with the onion stew and serve warm or cold.

Stuffed squids

4 servings

8 squids
2 cloves of garlic
9 ounces of breadcrumbs
fresh parsley
1 tablespoon of capers
2 tablespoons of grated pecorino cheese
1/2 cup extra virgin olive oil
salt and pepper TT

Clean and peel the squids, put out the heads, then wash them carefully, chop the legs and mix them with a mixture of minced capers, garlic and parsley; add the breadcrumbs, the pecorino cheese, salt and pepper and stir all together.
Add some oil to soften the mixture and then fill the squids. Close with sticks and put the stuffed squids in an oiled baking-pan. Sprinkle them with oil and salt, then bake them at 350° F for about 20 minutes.
If you like you can accompany the squids with cuttlefish ink sauce, obtained cooking the minced legs with a clove of garlic that will be put out after the cooking and a little of oil.
Add some wine and 1 glass of cuttlefish ink, season with salt and pepper, add some warm water and let cook for about 30 minutes.

Mackerel fillets "lardiati"

4 servings

4 big mackerels
3 cloves of garlic
fresh parsley
1/3 teaspoon oregano
8 tbsp extra virgin olive oil
5 tbsp vinegar
salt and pepper TT

Peel the garlic, crush and put it in a bowl. Add the oil, the vinegar, the minced parsley, the oregano, salt and pepper and mix all together. Clean and fillet the mackerels, add some salt. Roast the fish and then pour on top the prepared sauce and serve.

Dried cod "alla messinese" (typical of the zone of Messina)

4 servings

1 pound of softened dried cod fillets
1.2 pounds of potatoes
6 ounces of pitted green olives
2 ounces of capers
1 onion
1 clove of garlic
some celery
parsley
2 tablespoons of raisins
14 ounces of peeled tomatoes
1/2 cup extra virgin olive oil
1 cup flour
salt and pepper TT

Stir-fry a minced mixture of onion, parsley and celery in a large saucepan, with 5 tablespoons of oil and 1 clove of garlic (that you can remove). Add the chopped tomatoes, the capers and the sliced olives, stir and cook on a low flame for 10 minutes. In the meanwhile, stir-fry the potatoes, already peeled and sliced, with a little of oil; then drain them up and put together with the sauce. Heat some oil and stir-fry the skinned cod, already chopped and floured; then add it to the sauce and the rest of the ingredients. Pour one cup of hot water, season with salt and pepper and let simmer for about 1 hour, stirring occasionally. At the end of the coocking, add some minced parsley.

Swordfish soup "a ghiotta"

4 servings

4 slices of swordfish
1 onion
9 ounces of peeled tomatoes
1 tablespoon of capers
6 ounces of pitted green olives
fresh parsley
1 celery stalk with leaves
3 tbsp extra virgin olive oil
salt and pepper TT

Slice the onion and brown in a saucepan with oil and minced celery and parsley. Add the chopped tomatoes, the capers, the sliced olives, salt and pepper and let cook, at low heat for about 10 minutes. In the meanwhile clean and skin the fish, dry it up with kitchen paper and put it in the sauce. Cover with some tablespoons of sauce and go on cooking at low heat for 15 minutes.

"Matalotta" conger-eel

4 servings

2 pounds of filleted and chopped conger-eels
1 onion
some parsley
5 peeled tomatoes
3 tbsp extra virgin olive oil
salt and pepper TT

Clean and wash the eels, then dry and add some salt. Mince the onion and brown it with some oil in a saucepan, Add the chopped tomatoes, some parsley and let simmer for a couple of minutes. Pour a cup of hot water and let boil. Add a little of salt and the fish, go on cooking for no more than 10 minutes, on a low flame.

Tuna rissoles

4 servings

1 1/2 pounds of fresh tuna fish
1 egg
parsley
2 ounces of pine nuts
3 tbsp breadcrumbs
2 lemons
1 cup flour
1 cup extra virgin olive oil
salt and pepper TT

Leave the tuna in cold water for about 1/2 hour; then drain it up, dry and mince it.
Put it in a bowl and add the pine nuts, 1 egg, some salt and pepper, some minced parsley and 3 tablespoons of breadcrumbs.
Coat and knead well the the mixture till it is compact and homogenous. Add some more breadcrumbs if necessary.
With this mixture form little rissoles. Press them with hands, flour and fry them in hot oil.
Serve with lemon slices.

Breaded swordfish

4 servings

- **1 pound** of flour
- **7 ounces** of butter
- **1** egg
- **1** yolk
- **1** tablespoon of sugar
- **1** lemon
- **2 pounds** of sliced swordfish
- **10 ounces** of peeled tomatoes
- **2** zucchini
- **3 1/2** ounces of green olives
- **1** onion
- **1** tablespoon of capers
- some parsley
- some celery
- **9 tbsp** extra virgin olive oil
- salt and pepper TT

Sift the flour on the work top, add the chopped butter, 1 egg, 3 tablespoons of water, the sugar, the grated lemon peel, some salt and knead to obtain a homogenous mixture. Wrap it in some plastic film and leave in the fridge for 2 hours. Clean the zucchini; then slice and fry them. Brown the minced onion in a saucepan with 5 tablespoons of oil. Add the chopped tomatoes, the minced parsley, the capers, the sliced olives, some salt and pepper and simmer for a while. Add then the fish and go on cooking for 10 minutes, turning the slices to make them cook uniformly. Roll out the dough and form 4 rectangular sheets. Spread the swordfish and the fried zucchini on two sheets and close with the others sealing the rims with some beaten yolk. Use the rest of the dough to decorate. Swab the "wallets" with some beaten yolk and put in a baking-pan with greaseproof paper. Bake at 395° F for about 20 min.

Fried tuna semen

4 servings

- **1 1/2** ounces of cleaned tuna semen
- **1** cup flour
- **2** medium lemons
- **1** cup extra virgin olive oil
- salt TT

Cut the tuna semen in slices and flour the slices adding salt, then fry in plenty of hot oil. Once browned, strain and serve with lemon.

Drowned octopus

4 servings

2 pounds of octopuses
parsley, **1/2 bu.**
10 ounces of peeled tomatoes
1 clove of garlic
1/2 onion
3 tbsp dry white wine
3 tbsp extra virgin olive oil
salt and pepper TT

Stir-fry a mix of minced onion, parsley and garlic, with a little of oil. Add some wine and let evaporate, then add the chopped tomatoes and some salt and cook for 5 minutes. Add the octopuses, cover and let simmer at low heat.Once cooked the octopuses, add some salt if necessary and sprinkle with pepper.

Fried dried cod

4 servings

2 pounds of filleted and softened dried cod
1 cup flour
1 cup extra virgin olive oil
salt TT

Wash and dry the fish; then skin and chop it in little pieces.
Flour the fish slightly, and deep fry it in plenty of hot oil. Drain and sprinkle it with salt.
Serve the fish with lemon slices or, if you like, with mayonnaise seasoned with garlic and Cayenne pepper.

Marinated tuna

4 servings

- **4** thin slices of fresh tuna
- **10 ounces** of tomato pulp
- **1** onion
- **1** cup flour
- **1** cup white vinegar
- **8 tbsp** extra virgin olive oil
- **1 tbsp** sugar
- salt and pepper TT

Put the slices of fish in a bowl, pour 1 cup of water mixed with vinegar and let soak for about 1/2 hour. Then drain the tuna and dry it; flour and fry with some oil. Brown the sliced onion in a saucepan with some oil; add the tomato sauce, salt and pepper and let simmer for 15 minutes. Add the vinegar and a tablespoon of sugar and leave the fish to gain flavour. Put then the fish in the saucepan with the sauce and let cook for 5 minutes.

Salted sea bass

4 servings

- **4** sea basses
- **4** cloves of garlic (optional)
- **1** sprig of thyme (optional)
- **6 pounds** of sea salt
- pepper

Clean, wash and dry the fish. Sprinkle with pepper and, if desired, put a clove of garlic and some thyme inside the cavity of each fish. Put the salt in a bowl and and stir in 1 1/2 cups of water to obtain a thick mixture. (Add water if necessary). Fill 4 baking pans with half of the mixture making thick layers. Put a sea bass in each baking pan and cover with the remaining salt making a solid cover without any hole. Heat oven at 390° F and bake the fish for about 15 minutes. Serve the fish with a mixture of oil and lemon or mayonnaise.

MEAT

Beef, traditionally belonging to the Sunday meal, rarely appears in the Sicilian food. Frequent droughts and dry pastures have not encouraged large grazing animals. Popular cuisine is rich in recipes with rabbit, lamb, kid and pork instead. Breaded roast and Sicilian roulades are recent achievements. Wealth has introduced veal in the Sicilian diet, a type of meat almost unknown one hundred years ago in the island. An exception is the meat roll, probably of French origin, present in the Sicilian cuisine since long ago. Kid and lamb, once linked to the Easter period, has become today a valid alternative to red meat.

Sicilian roulades

4 servings

12 thin slices of veal
1 cup of breadcrumbs
2 tablespoons of grated pecorino cheese
1 tablespoon of raisins
1 tablespoon of pine nuts
1 onion
fresh parsley
8 bay leaves in halves
1/2 cup extra virgin olive oil
salt and pepper TT

Mince and brown the onion in some oil. Add the breadcrumbs and toast them a little. Cool down and put in a bowl, add the pecorino, the raisins, the pine nuts, the parsley and some salt and pepper, soften the mixture with oil. Pound the meat with a meat mallet. Spread the prepared mixture on the meat slices and roll up every slice making roulades. Add some oil and then cover the roulades with breadcrumbs. Thread on skewer alternating roulades with pieces of onion and bay leaves and bake at 350° F with some oil for about 20 minutes.

Meat roll

4 servings

veal rump in 1 slice of about 1 pound
10 1/2 ounces ground beef
1 egg
3 1/2 ounces breadcrumbs
1 tuft parsley
1 1/2 ounces grated caciocavallo
(or pecorino)
1 tbsp pine nuts
2 thin slices of mortadella
1 1/2 ounces of salami in slices
3 cups of tomato sauce
5 tbsp red Marsala wine
1 medium onion
2 boiled carrots
2 tbsp extra virgin olive oil
1/2 teaspoon sugar
1 ounce butter

Put the ground beef in a bowl, add the bread crumbs, the ground parsley, the egg, the cheese, the pine nuts, a pinch of salt and a dash of pepper and mix well. Roll out the slice of meat on a chopping board and pound it with a meat mallet; sprinkle with salt and pepper. Make layers with the mortadella, the salami and the ground beef mixture. Top with the boiled carrots. Roll up the slice making a big roulade and secure with kitchen thread. Brown in a large saucepan with the butter and some oil. Add the wine and let evaporate. Dissolve a cup of warm water in the tomato sauce and add the chopped onion. Add a pinch of salt, the sugar and a dash of pepper and cook on moderate flame for about 1 hour, turning the meat over a couple of times. When cooked remove the roulade from the sauce and cool until warm. Slice and put on a platter. Trickle with the sauce and serve.

Breaded roasted meat

4 servings

4 slices of veal
fresh parsley
5 tbsp extra virgin olive oil
salt and pepper TT

Roll out the slices of meat on a chopping board and pound them with a meat mallet; deep them in a mixture of oil, salt and pepper then in the breadcrumbs seasoned with ground parsley, roast the meat in hot grill.

Kid with almonds

4 servings

3 pounds of kid in pieces
7 ounces of peeled almonds
1 onion
10 ounces of ripe tomatoes
fresh parsley
3 tbsp extra virfgin olive oil
salt and pepper TT

Mince the almonds coarsely. Wash and dry the kid. Brown the chopped onion with a little of oil.

Add the meat and stir fry it on a low flame; add then the peeled and chopped tomatoes, a little of salt and pepper and let gain flavour. Pour a cup of hot water, half of almonds and minced parsley. Stir well and cover, at low heat for less than 1 hour adding some tablespoons of water from time to time.
At the end sprinkle with the rest of almonds.

Glazed kid

4 servings

1,5 kg of kid in pieces
600 g of potatoes
4 ripe tomatoes
1 big onion
1 bay leaf
fresh parsley
3 tbsp dry Marsala wine
5 tbsp extra virgin olive oil
salt and pepper TT

Barbecued lamb cutlets

4 servings

8 lamb cutlets
1 bay leaf
3 garlic cloves
2 lemons
oregano
5 tbsp extra virgin olive oil
salt and pepper TT

Wash and dry the kid, then stir-fry it in a saucepan with the sliced onion, the bay leaf and the oil. Once browned, add the Marsala wine and let it evaporate. Add the chopped potatoes and let flavour for a couple of minutes; add the peeled and chopped tomatoes, the parsley and some salt and pepper.

Cover with hot water and let cook for about 1 hour.

Chop the garlic and put it in a bowl. Add the lemon juice, the extra virgin olive oil, some oregano and pepper and beat all together with a fork to obtain a sauce.

Add this sauce to the cutlets and leave them to soak for at least 1 hour. Then drain the meat and roast it on a hot barbecue.

Add salt only at the end.

Sweet and sour rabbit

4 servings

- **1** rabbit in pieces
- **1** bay leaf
- **1** medium onion
- **1** stalk of celery
- **2** cloves garlic
- **1 pound** peeled tomatoes
- **1/3** teaspoon oregano
- fresh basil
- **1/2** cup extra virgin olive oil
- **8 tbsp** white vinegar
- **1/2** tbsp sugar
- salt, pepper TT

Crush the garlic in a mortar with the leaves of basil and a pinch of salt. Add the chopped tomatoes and mix until well blended. Pour the sauce in a bowl and add 6 tablespoons of oil, some oregano and a little pepper. Boil the rabbit for 5 minutes with a bay leaf and the lemon rind; drain and dry the rabbit with kitchen paper. Put then the meat in a saucepan and add the remaining oil, some bay leaves and browned onion and celery. Sauté the meat, stirring often and adding occasionally 1 spoon of hot water. Once stir-fried add the vinegar melted with 1/2 tablespoon of sugar and let evaporate, covering the saucepan. Take the lid off only a few minutes before switching off the flame and serve the preparation sprinkled with the tomato "pesto", prepared in advance.

Sausage sauce with pork rinds

4 servings

- **1 1/2 pounds** of sausage in big chunks
- **7 ounces** of fresh pork rinds
- **3** cups of tomato sauce
- **1** bay leaf
- **1** medium onion
- **1 tbsp** of raisins
- **3 tbsp** extra virgin olive oil
- **1/3** teaspoon of sugar
- salt and pepper TT

Singe the pork rinds and wash them carefully with water; then boil and drain them. Cook the sausage in a pan with some water for about 5 minutes, poking the sausage with a wooden skewer. Put the peeled onion, the tomato sauce, the raisins, the bay leaf, some salt, sugar and pepper, in a saucepan with some oil and let simmer for about 10 minutes. Add the sliced pork rinds and the sausage and for 1 hour on a low flame.

SWEETS

*Ricotta is the queen of creams in
the island's sweets, is often
accompanied by chocolate or
pumpkin preserve in the filling of
specialties as "St. Joseph's
sfincioni", the "cassatelle". The
classical traditional sweets,
ricotta cannoli and cakes.
Inherited from the Spaniards, an
infinity of sweets: from the
"cubbaita" (a nougat of sesame
or almonds) to "buccellati"
(biscuits stuffed with a mixture of
dried figs); from watermelon
sherbet to "biancomangiare".
Authentic delicacies are the
almond-based sweets: almond
paste with its extraordinary
shapes, semifreddo (soft ice-
cream), and nougats.
The simplicity of the Sicilian
cuisine is enriched by the
elaborate sweets originating the
foreign occupations in Sicily.*

"Cassata" (Sicilian regional cake with ricotta)

8 servings

For the sponge cake:
4 eggs
2/3 cup of superfine granulated sugar
2 cups of flour
1 ounce of baking powder
1/2 lemon
5 tbsp Marsala or vermouth
1/16 tsp. salt
butter and flour for the cake-tin
For the filling:
17 1/2 ounces of sheep ricotta
1/4 teaspoon vanillin extract
2 ounces of diced candied fruit
2 ounces dark chocolate in flakes
1/16 tsp. salt
For the almond paste:
9 ounces of shelled blanched almonds
1 1/2 cups of caster sugar (superfine granulated)
3 drops of almond extract
1 pinch of vanillin
green food colouring
5 tbsp of water
For the icing and the decoration:
1 1/3 cups of caster sugar
2 egg whites
1 tbsp of lemon juice
1 pound mixed candied fruit

For the cake beat the egg whites stiff with a pinch of salt.

In another bowl cream the yolks with the sugar. Sift the flour, the baking soda add a couple of tbsp. of the stiff whites and combine.
Season with some grated lemon peel.
Add the remaining egg whites and pour the pastry in a baking-pan greased with butter and floured. Bake at 380° F for about 40 minutes. Set out to cool. Mince the almonds little by little in a food processor or coffee grinder. Put in a mixer; add 9 ounces of caster sugar, the vanillin and the almond essence, dissolved in 5 tbsp. of water and beat. When combined put on a marble board sprinkled with caster sugar and combine with a few drops of water in which a drop of green food colouring has been dissolved. Wrap in film and store in the refrigerator.
Beat the ricotta until it is smooth cream, and add the chocolate and the candied fruit.
Cover with transparent film, and refrigerate.
Cover the rims with the almond pastry, rolled out 1/4 in. thick and as large as the rims. You can alternate strips of almond pastry with strips of cake or cover the rims with an entire strip of almond pastry. Cover the bottom of the mould with slices of cake 1/2 in. thick and sprinkled with Marsala or sweet vermouth mixed with a little water. Now pour in the filling, and cover again with cake slices sprinkled with liquor.
Cover with a dish the same diameter as the mould and press a little, cool in the refrigerator for 20 min. Turn the mould upside down onto a dish and remove the transparent film.

"Cassatelle" with ricotta

8 servings

4 cups flour
3/4 cup of granulated sugar
1/4 cup glass of extra virgin olive oil
1 tbsp of brandy
1 lemon
1 pound of ricotta
2 ounces of dark chocolate
1/4 teaspoon cinnamon
1 egg white
2 tbsp caster sugar
2 cups vegetable oil
1/4 teaspoon salt

Beat the egg whites with the caster sugar for about 10 minutes to obtain a cream and mix the grated lemon. Cover the cake with this icing and spread with a spatula covering the rims too. Let it dry up and decorate with candied fruit. Decorate sides with the remaining icing using a pastry bag with a small, smooth opening. Cool down in fridge for a few hours before serving.

Make a soft dough mixing the flour with half of the sugar, 2 tbsp of lemon juice, the brandy, the olive oil and a pinch of salt, adding water if necessary.
Cover and let rest for about 30 minutes.
Mix the ricotta with the remaining sugar, the chocolate chips and a pinch of cinnamon.
Roll out the dough and cut some pieces in oval shape with a pastry cutter or a glass.
Spoon dollops of the mixture at the center of the disks. Brush the edges with beaten egg whites mixed with water and fold the filling inside forming raviolis. Fry the "cassatelle" in hot vegetable oil; drip on paper towel, sprinkle with caster sugar and serve warm.

St. Joseph "sfinge" (kind of doughnuts filled with ricotta)

8 servings

- **1 1/2** cups flour
- **2 ounces** of butter
- **3/4** cup of superfine granulated sugar
- **4** eggs
- **1/2 tbsp** of baking powder
- **14 ounces** of ricotta
- **2 tbsp** of chocolate, chopped
- **3 ounces** candied orange peels
- **2** cups vegetable oil
- **1/4** teaspoon salt

Boil the water together with the butter, 1 tbsp of sugar and some salt. Remove from fire and pour in the flour and stir well. Cook the batter till it detaches from the saucepan rims, let it cool and add the baking powder, stirring continuously. Once the batter is soft, add the eggs one by one. Cover it with a cloth and let it leaven for about 1 hour. Take 2-3 spoons of batter for each doughnut and fry them in deep hot oil. Once they are swollen and browned, drain and put them on a paper towel. Mix the ricotta with the remaining sugar and the chocolate chips. When the doughnuts have cooled down spread the cream on the fried "sfinge" and decorate with the candied orange peel.

"Cotognata"

- **2 pounds** peeled diced apples
- **2 pounds** caster sugar
- **1** lemon
- **2 tbsp** vegetable oil

Put the apples in a saucepan and add the lemon cut to pieces; cover with water and cook until soft. Remove the lemon and drain the apples, and push through a sieve. In a casserole, add the sugar and cook for 1 hour, stirring frequently.
When thick enough remove from flame and pour in a mould, slightly greased with the vegetable oil. Dry until firm.

"Buccellati" (Christmas biscuits)

8 servings

- **4** cups flour
- **3/4** cup of caster sugar
- **5 ounces** of margarine
- **1** small bag of yeast powder
- **4 tbsp** of honey
- **14 ounces** of dried figs
- **2 ounces** of shelled blanched almonds
- **1/4** teaspoon extract of vanillin
- **1** orange
- **2 tbsp** caster sugar
- **1/4** teapoon cinnamon
- **1** clove
- **2 tbsp** caster sugar

Mix the flour with: the sugar, margarine, two tbsp of the honey, a pinch of vanillin, the yeast and 1/2 cup of cold water. Wrap the mixture in transparent film and leave it to cool in refrigerator for 30 minutes. While waiting, mince the figs in a food processor, with the almonds, grated orange peel cinnamon and 1 clove. Place in a saucepan, add the honey and cook for a few minutes Add two tablespoons of water. Remove from flame and cool. Remove the dough from the refrigerator and roll out the dough to 1/2 inch. Cut it into rectangles of 2 x 4 inch. Place in the center of each a tablespoon of the fig and honey mixture. and roll the pasta, in the shape of tubes. Score on 3-5 points on the same side and fold in crescent shape. Place the buccellatis on a baking-pan with oven paper, sprinkle with decorative candies and cook at 455 F. for 20 minutes. Cool biscuits and sprinkle with powdered sugar.

Watermelon sherbet

8 servings

- **2 pounds** watermelon pulp
- **3 1/2 ounces** of corn starch
- **1** cup of caster sugar
- **1/4** teaspoon vanillin

Sieve the watermelon pulp. Place the juice in a bowl, and dissolve the corn starch in the melon juice. Add the sugar and stirring on a low flame let it thicken.
Add the vanillin and pour all in a wet mould. Leave in the refrigerator for one day before serving.

"Cannoli"(pastry tubes filled with ricotta)

Makes 20 cannoli

For the rolls:
2 1/3 cups flour
1 tbsp of powdered bitter cocoa
1 tbsp of caster sugar
1 1/2 ounces of butter
1 egg white
1 tbsp sweet Marsala wine
salt
2 cups vegetable oil
For the cream:
2 pounds sheep ricotta
6 1/3 ounces of caster sugar
1/2 teaspoon vanilla extract
2 tbsp chipped dark chocolate
5 ounces diced candied orange peels
salt TT

Soften the butter to room temperature. Make a smooth dough with the flour, butter, eggs, sugar, cocoa, wine and salt adding the necessary water. Put the pastry in the transparent film and leave it in the refrigerator for about 1 hour. Now in a bowl mix the ricotta with the sugar, a teaspoon of vanilla essence and a pinch of salt. Roll out the dough and cut some pieces in oval shape; then roll them up around the special aluminium tubes, sealing the edges together with the beaten white of the egg with some drops of water. Deep fry the rolls with the tubes in hot oil until brown, drain them on paper towel, slip the aluminium tubes out only when the fried rolls are completely cold. Add a couple of tablespoons of chocolate chips to the ricotta cream. Fill the pastry tubes with the ricotta mixture and sprinkle with powdered sugar. Decorate, if desired, with candied orange peels.

"Biancomangiare"

8 servings

4 1/4 cups of milk
3 1/2 ounces of corn starch
5 1/2 ounces of caster sugar

Dissolve the corn starch in 2 cups of the milk and heat. then add sugar and the remaining milk, thicken stirring on a low flame. Pour in wet little moulds and put in the fridge for at least 5 hours. Once cold, sprinkle with minced almonds.
Topping variation: mix 2.2 pounds of pureed fruit (apricots, peaches, strawberries) with a syrup made from 3 1/2 ounces of caster sugar and water. Simmer until a veil appears on the surface. Sieve and flavor with 2 –3 tbsp of orange liqueur.

"Cubbaita"

8 servings

1 1/2 cups of caster sugar
3 1/2 ounces of honey
10 ounces of sesame seeds

Pour sugar and honey in a casserole and place on medium heat. Stir with a wooden spoon and heat until mixture turns caramel color. Add the sesame seeds and keep cooking for a few minutes. Turn out the prepared mixture on greased marble counter top and spread to a thickness of about 1/8 inch, using half lemon stuck on a fork or a well-greased knife. Cool the cubbaita and cut to bits using a greased knife. Desired shapes can be cut out using a cookie cutter.

Fruit of Martorana

Makes about 4 pounds of sweets

2 pounds sliced blanched almonds
5 cups of caster sugar
1/2 teaspoon extract of vanilla
6 drops extract of bitter almonds
1/4 teaspoon ground cinnamon
4 tbsp corn starch
food coloring

Mince the almonds in food processor with little sugar and set aside. Place 3/4 ounces of water in a saucepan; add sugar and set on moderate flame, stirring constantly. Melt sugar completely, add the puree of almonds, 1/2 teaspoon of extract of vanilla, 6 drops of extract of bitter almonds and a pinch of cinnamon and stir the mixture with a wood spoon, until it easily separates from the sides of the casserole. Transfer the mix to an oiled marble counter top to cool enough to knead by hand. While still soft, divide it into 5-6 portions and set aside for 24 hours. Refine the pasta of almonds with a pasta machine to a desired thickness. Cut out into desired shapes or press the prepared candy into special stencils sprinkled with corn starch. Remove the "Martorana" fruit with a lot of care and let harden for 1 day. Finally, color the sweets and let dry.

Almond nougat

2 pounds of caster sugar
3 1/2 ounces of glucose
14 ounces of shelled blanched almonds
wafers, enough to cover mould

Toast the almonds and let cool. Put the sugar in a casserole. Add the glucose and 9 ounces of water and cook, on medium heat, mixing slowly with a wooden spoon. Skim with a perforated ladle and dampen the walls of the saucepan with a wet brush. After about 15 minutes, dip a wooden spoon in the caramel, if a thread is formed that can be broken immediately, remove from flame. Pour the mixture on a slightly greased marble counter top and then work with a spatula or a wooden shovel. Bring the edges of it toward the center, knead to the point it becomes white and soft. Stir in the coarsely chopped almonds. Transfer the mix to the special mould covered with the wafers and level the surface. Cover with other wafers and let the nougat harden. Remove from mould.

Almond "Semifreddo" (Italian soft ice cream)

8 servings

12 1/3 ounces of shelled blanched almonds
2 cups whipped cream
1 1/2 cups of caster sugar
4 eggs
7 ounces of dark chocolate
1 tbsp of butter
3 tbsp milk
salt

Pour 7 ounces of sugar in a saucepan with one tablespoon of water and simmer for a couple of minutes. Add the almonds and stir until the sugar coats the almonds. Put on a greased marble board and separate almonds and let them cool. Separate the eggs. Beat egg whites stiff with a pinch of salt. Beat yolks and remaining sugar until smooth. Mince the almonds and add to the eggs, keeping 4-5 tbsp aside for the decorations. Combine the whipped cream and the eggs. Pour the cream mixture into a mould (or several little moulds) and keep in the freezer for at least 8 hours. Dissolve the chocolate, in bain marie, in the butter and a few tablespoons of milk and simmer until smooth. Remove "semifreddo" from mould and top with the melted chocolate and the minced almonds.

Index